The Basics of Harmonica Playing

An extensive guide for the beginner harmonica player

Table of Contents

Introduction 1
   What this book will teach you. 1
   What is a harmonica? 2
   Different types of harmonicas. 6

How to Select and Purchase the Correct Harmonica 9

How to hold your harmonica 13
   The open cup grip. 13
   The closed Cup grip. 14

Playing Single Notes 15
   The pucker method. 16
   The tongue block method. 17

Playing Chords 19
   Compacted chord tongue block. 22
   Split chord tongue block. 23

Enhancing the Sound with Your Tongue 25
   The tongue lift. 25
   The tongue slap. 26
   The tongue rake. 27
   The pull off. 28
   The chord hammer. 28

    The shimmer. 29

Bending the Notes 31

    Bending during inhalation. 33

    Bending during exhalation. 34

Playing the Harmonica in Many Keys 37

Bringing It All Together 41

Introduction

What this book will teach you.

This book aims to teach you – as a beginner harmonica player– the basics of the harmonica and what you need to know to support your own development of the skill. This book is a general guide and introduction to learning an instrument used on almost every corner of the globe. This book also aims to help develop your overall knowledge and skill of music through the instrument called the harmonica.

More specifically this book will focus on developing correct technique and skills needed to successfully control the instrument and manipulate it to create the sounds that are desired by the player. Techniques such as playing single notes and chords; enhancing sound through the use of the tongue; bending notes; and playing in different keys will be discussed throughout the book and practiced using certain techniques. This book will also take you through the controlled steps of learning different techniques. These steps also act as exercises which you can come back to for constant practice. The book will also bring all of the knowledge learned together for a final section that will round up everything this book has presented.

What is a harmonica?

What type of instrument is it?

A harmonica is classified as a wind instrument. A wind instrument is an instrument that requires a player to blow over or into the instrument to produce a sound. A harmonica makes use of resonating reeds to produce sounds. The harmonica is quite a special wind instrument as players are able to produce sounds when breathing both in and out of the harmonica – a wind instrument that responds to inhalation and exhalation. The harmonica originates from Asia, more specifically China, where it evolved from an instrument, called the sheng. The idea of this mouth organ then traveled to Europe where it started to evolve into the forms that we find the instrument in today. Harmonica companies were growing at an increasing rate during the 19th century and manufacturers were sending their harmonicas to America – a country that took to the instrument very quickly.

What does it look like?

A harmonica most often looks like a rectangularly shaped instrument which has 6 flat sided surfaces. The narrower and longer side section placed against the mouth usually has a number of holes which act as airways that make contact with reeds. The opposite side of the mouth piece is usually barred with the same material that the harmonica is cased with, still allowing space at the receiving end for sound to escape. Some different types of harmonicas have added on features such as side buttons, or slides, which can be pushed to alter the notes played. A harmonica is small enough to hold up to the mouth with both hands but can also sit on a holder which allows the player to use his hands for another instrument. Harmonicas were traditionally made with wood but now can be found having been made of metal or plastic. Wooden harmonicas are considered to be highly priced but the material is still used today to produce unique sounds.

The different parts of the harmonica.

There is way more to a harmonica that can just be seen on the outside of it. There are quite a few parts that make up the harmonica and help produce the sounds that it plays. There are five main parts of the harmonica that make it what it is. These parts are the comb; the reed plates; the cover plates; windsavers; and a mouthpiece. Different types of harmonicas have other add-on features but these five main parts are typically seen in all harmonicas in order for them to work.

Let's take a more in depth look at the parts that make up a harmonica.

A diagram at the end of this section will help you see where these parts sit on the instrument.

- The comb

    The comb is the main body of the harmonica and is found in the middle of the instrument. The comb is fitted with reed plates on the top and bottom of the harmonica's chambers/holes in which a player's air travels through, striking the reeds and producing a certain pitch. The amount of chambers found depends on what type of harmonica it is and the size of its scale. The comb is usually made out of metal or plastic. Combs were originally made from wood but stress over time caused fractures and cracks. Wood also expands which can affect chamber size and ultimately set the harmonica off-tune. The comb is the base on which the instrument is built.

- Reed plates

Wind instruments often make use of reeds and a harmonica is no different. Harmonicas are made with two reed plates. One reed plate sits on top of the comb while the other sits below both having access to an airflow chamber. Reed plates are usually made from metals or plastic and have reeds fitted on them. Reeds are made from the same material as the reed plate and are fitted onto the reed plate with screws or by welding. Each chamber in the comb is home to two reeds which are facing opposite each other. One reed plate is made to produce sound when a player blows on the harmonica while the other reed plate, in the same chamber, produces sound when a player draws breath on the harmonica. This makes it possible to have two reeds in one chamber without the collision of two notes at the same time. Reeds are fitted specifically to produce certain notes when played by a harmonica player and are pitched in scales. Both the reeds and the reed plate can be replaced which is a must when your harmonica is going out of tune.

- Cover plates.

    A harmonica has two cover plates. Cover plates are bolted onto the comb and on the outside of the reed plates. They protect and hold the whole of the harmonica together. Traditional harmonicas have cover plates that are made out of wood, metal or plastic. It is believed that the type of material used as a cover can change the quality of sound heard from the harmonica. Tone can also be affected by the type of material that is used as a cover plate for a harmonica. Cover plates are what makes your harmonica look good so they are usually finished with a strong coat of something attractive to the eye.

- Windsavers.

    Windsavers are small strips of plastic which are glued to the reeds on the reed plate. They act almost as air flaps. The position of the windsaver determines whether the strip opens up or closes during inhalation or exhalation. Windsavers are only found in some harmonicas that cannot block certain reeds through inhalation or exhalation. Windsavers are used to block airflow to specific reeds during inhalation or exhalation. Windsavers are used when there are leakages of air out of the reed that is not supposed to be in use – remember that this reed would be sharing a chamber with the reed that is in use. Windsavers prevent leakages of air from happening and restrict the harmonica to playing one note at a time from each chamber in use.

- The mouth piece.

    The mouth piece is fitted onto one of the narrow and long sides of the harmonica. It is precisely fitted to allow a pathway for air into the chambers of the comb. The mouthpiece is the part of the harmonica that is pressed against the mouth and given airflow. The inward curve or decline of the mouthpiece compared to the rest of the harmonica allows for a better slide of the lips when a player is moving around and playing with notes.

Different types of harmonicas.

There are many types of harmonicas which are found across the globe. There are some you may encounter and some you may not. It is useful to know the types of harmonicas there are as some may interest you in the future.

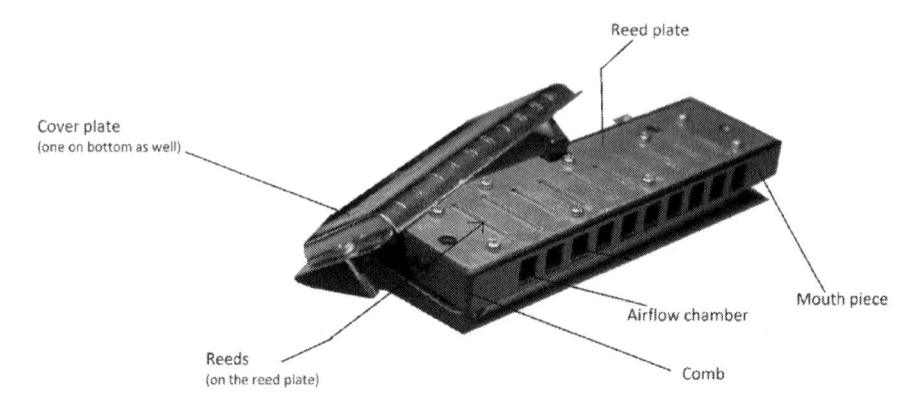

Diatonic harmonicas; chromatic harmonicas; orchestral harmonicas; tremelo harmonicas; ChengGong harmonicas; and electric harmonicas are some popular harmonicas used around the world. There are however two types of harmonicas that are more suitable for beginners.

These two popular beginner harmonicas are the chromatic harmonica and the diatonic harmonica.

- Chromatic Harmonica

    A chromatic harmonica follows the chromatic scale which is a western scale. The chromatic harmonica can be made with eight, ten, twelve, fourteen or sixteen holes. You can find some harmonicas with more holes than sixteen but these are not as commonly seen. A chromatic harmonica has a slide (side button) which can push the played note a semi tone up. A 12-hole chromatic harmonica is considered to be the best for beginner chromatic harmonica players as it is able to play every key of the chromatic scale.

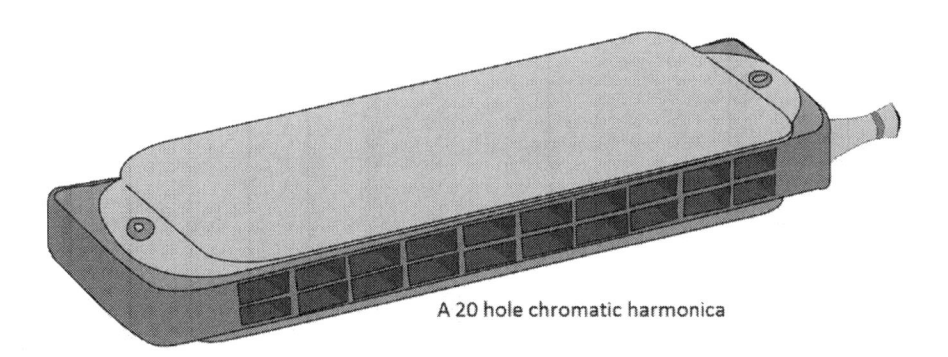

    A 20 hole chromatic harmonica

- Diatonic Harmonica

    This harmonica is considered to be the best and easiest harmonica to learn on. The diatonic harmonica can only play in one key unlike the chromatic harmonica and does not have a slide. Diatonic harmonicas are common and easy to find. Diatonic harmonicas are usually found with ten holes but other variations can be found. It is common to see most beginners owning this harmonica and specifically one which has been tuned to in the key of C. A ten-hole diatonic harmonica is definitely a strong recommendation for the beginner harmonica player even more so than a chromatic harmonica.

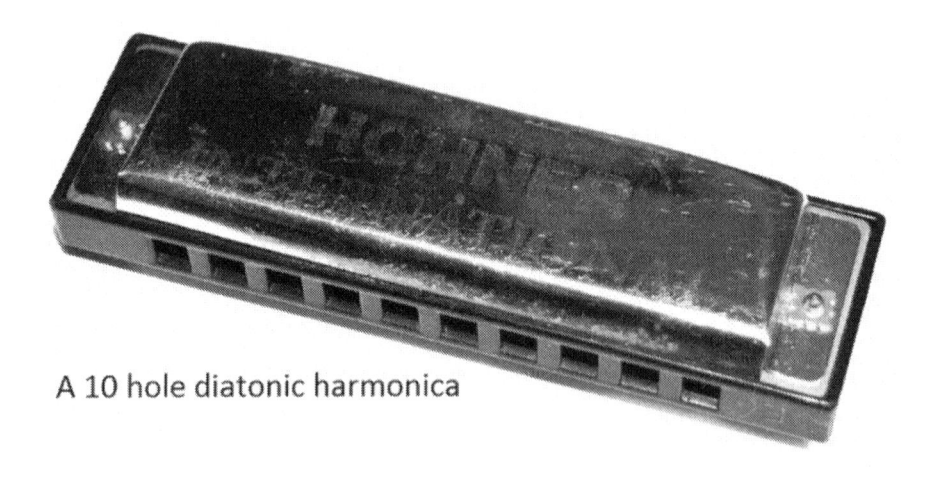

A 10 hole diatonic harmonica

How to Select and Purchase the Correct Harmonica

It is very advisable for the beginner harmonica player to start off with purchasing either a diatonic harmonica or chromatic harmonica – more so for a diatonic harmonica. People looking to begin playing the harmonica should think of the time they will put into learning the instrument. If you are serious and enthusiastic about learning, it may be advisable to purchase a chromatic harmonica as it will offer more room to grow than a diatonic harmonica would. This is due to the chromatic harmonica easily being able to play in different keys as well as being more of a versatile type of harmonica. The diatonic harmonica is strongly recommended for beginner players who just want to learn the instrument casually and acquire the skill at their own pace. Finding harmonicas are quite an easy task and it should not be hard finding one when you have the time.

Where you go to find a harmonica depends on three main things. How much you are willing to pay, the method of purchase you prefer and what exactly you are looking for. Most musical instrument shops will have a few types of harmonicas in stock. Bigger musical instrument shops seem to have more of a variety of harmonicas to choose from. Trying to find specific harmonicas with certain numbers of holes might mean having to order through a musical instrument shop who will ship it in for you. Online purchase is another option but it is advisable to order from reliable sellers. The internet is where you can also order more exotic harmonicas such as the ChengGong.

Pricing a harmonica.

Pricing a harmonica depends on where you buy it from. Some musical instrument stores can charge a bit more for their harmonicas to make a profit but at least a buyer will know they are getting quality. Buying online might be cheaper but it can be risky concerning the quality of the product as well as carrying the possibility of shipping charges.

A good price for a great quality diatonic harmonica can cost between $25 to $60 U.S - Where a good price for a high-quality chromatic harmonica can cost between $100 to $200 U.S.

Tips for the buy.

It is good to test your harmonica before purchase by just giving it a quick play, even if you don't know how. A harmonica is a good choice for you if you like the sound of it when you test it and if it feels comfortable. Just remember to enjoy the experience and find a harmonica you know you will fall in love with. Beginner harmonica players who wish to purchase a diatonic harmonica should remember to decide which key they wish their harmonica to play in, especially if they are playing with a music group or band.

Different brands of harmonica.

There are many brands of harmonica out there but some out trump others. Brands such as Suzuki, Hohner, Bushman, Seydel, and Oskar are all popular brands that should provide you with high-quality harmonicas. Take your time to look around and find the harmonica ideal for you.

Take all of this information into consideration when buying a harmonica and remember to find one that will inspire you to learn.

How to hold your harmonica

We can now take a look at a more practical aspect of learning the harmonica. It is crucial to apply the correct technique from the start to develop your skills healthily. Early bad habits on an instrument can lead to incorrect technique later on. Some types of harmonicas require slightly different holding techniques but this section will teach you the grips for the diatonic harmonica which is the more popular harmonica for beginners.

The open cup grip.

The open cup grip is a common technique first used by beginners to help get the feel of the instrument. This grip requires your left hand to clamp the harmonica from its left side covering the top base of the harmonica with your fingers and the bottom base with your thumb. The right hand is placed upright along the right side of the harmonica with the player's fingers pointing upwards. This technique helps the player get a firm grip on the harmonica which is needed. Take a look at the picture below to better understand an open cup grip.

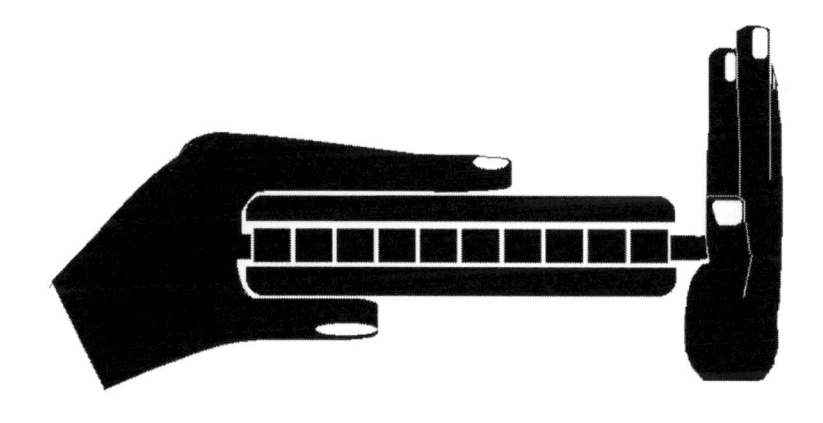

The closed Cup grip.

The closed cup grip is another common grip used by beginners and can actually help enhance the sound of your harmonica. Your left-hand does the same as it would do if you were playing an open cup grip. Your left hand is to clamp the harmonica from its left side covering the top base of the harmonica with your fingers and the bottom base with your thumb. Your right hand is where the closed cup grip differs from an open cup grip. Your right hand should now have your thumb pressed against the right side of the harmonica. Your right hand should then wrap around the front of the harmonica with your fingers clamping down on your left-hand fingers.

A closed cup grip can allow you to add great sound effects to your harmonica, shaking and waving your right hand can produce a vibrato sound while playing for example. Take a look at the picture below to better understand a closed cup grip.

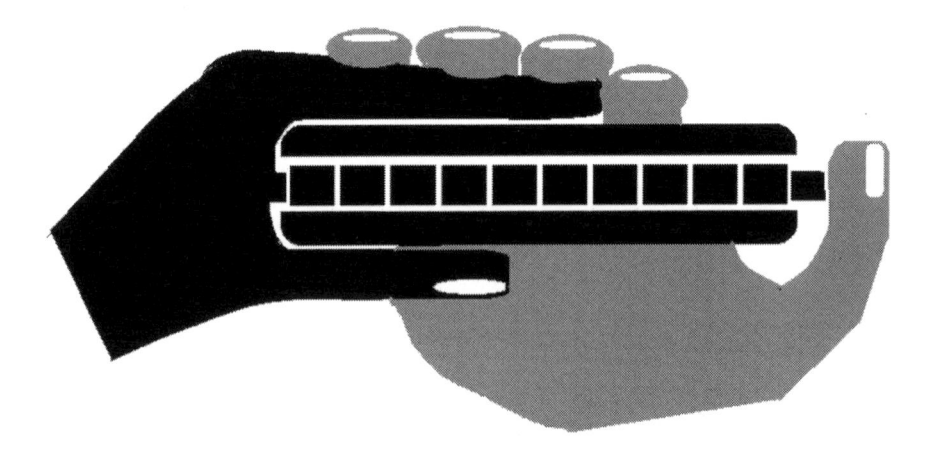

Playing Single Notes

What is a single note?

Some of you who are reading this section might be asking what exactly a single note is. We can break the two words down and define them as the singular. The word 'single' means only one and no other while the word note – in musical terms – is the word for the markings found in music literature that presents the pitch as well the as duration of an audible sound. This pretty much describes exactly what a single note is. A single note is one note played at one pitch for a certain duration of time. The duration of time played, in this case, will not affect the development of the technique which makes it unimportant and unnecessary to touch on. This section's aim is to help you develop the technique of playing a single note on the harmonica. These techniques apply to most, if not all types of harmonicas.

How to play a single note.

A single note on the harmonica is played by isolating one hole and exhaling or inhaling to produce a sound. There are two techniques that are commonly used to play a single note on the harmonica. One being the pucker method and the other being the tongue block method.

You should be familiar with your harmonica by now and have made a sound or two through exhalation or inhalation. If not, give it a go and have a bit of fun.

Now it is time to focus on your lips. Mouth techniques used while playing wind instruments are called embouchures. Here are two embouchures which are definitely useful when trying to play a single note on the harmonica.

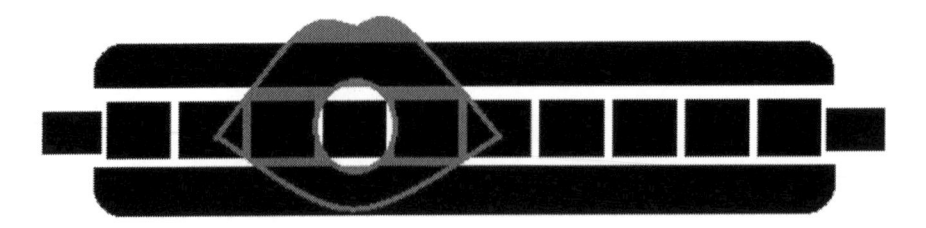

The pucker method.

The pucker method is a method of lip positioning on the harmonica. The idea is to shape your lips as if you are a kissing or whistling and place it over the hole you wish to play. Take a look below.

The idea behind this method is to eliminate air flow reaching any other hole on your harmonica and isolate the hole you wish to play at the same time. This will help ensure that you hear one distinct note that you may play for the duration of time you want. Try practice this as often as you can to improve the strength of the muscles around your lips.

Tricks and tips…

The pucker method may seem easy but many beginner harmonica players often struggle with learning the technique. Here are a few tricks and tips to help you develop this embouchure.

- Tilting the harmonica upwards while keeping your lips puckered can help with playing a single note. This trick helps make that gap for airflow to other holes a lot smaller. Once you start improving you can tilt the harmonica further down to an angle where it is more comfortable.

- This method can be tiring for the muscles around your mouth. This can be improved though by giving your mouth a workout in your spare time. Whistling is a good work out for this technique and whistling for at least one minute a day can help strengthen your mouth muscles.

The tongue block method.

The tongue block method is an embouchure where the player uses his tongue and the end of his mouth to block holes on the harmonica and isolate one to play a single note. The tongue should sit in the left side of the mouth, leaving a gap for air on the right side of the mouth. A good thing about this embouchure is that you can block multiple holes at once with the tongue.

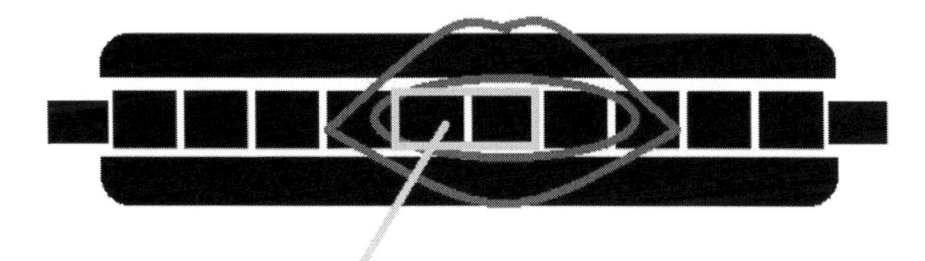

Tongue blocking two holes.

This embouchure may be difficult to get right at first but it is not as tough as one may think. Visualizing what is happening in your mouth helps a lot with finding the right spots for your tongue. Hearing what is happening is also obviously key to success. Just remember to take your time and get these single notes right before moving on.

Playing Chords

The tongue is able to create chords on the harmonica. Chords are two or more harmonizing notes/holes that are being played together simultaneously to create a whole sound.

To fully understand what a chord is on a harmonica it is crucial to know what exactly is happening in a chord.

A chord works with notes that are found in musical scales.

What is a scale?

There are a few types of scales found on different harmonicas. A scale is a set of defined notes or pitches which can ascend and descend. Ultimately providing the basic platform in which musicians can base their music on. These pitches are named after the first seven letters of the Roman alphabet, these pitches are A, B, C, D, E, F and G and are portrayed through musical notation which is considered to be the universal language for music.

Diatonic harmonicas make use of the diatonic scale which consists of these seven different pitches also known as notes. Each pitch has its own scale which starts with a note that the actual key focuses on.

As an example – the C major diatonic scale would be played as follows, C – D – E – F – G – A – B.

Every pitch/note was used but in a particular order which makes it a C major scale.

Knowing this makes it easier to understand chords as a chord is just a selection of notes/pitches in a scale played together to create a fuller sound.

The root chord of C major is C – E – G and only consists of three notes. Here is an example of a scale descending and ascending in C major. Look at the scale of C major below to help you find a pattern with its root chord of C – E – G.

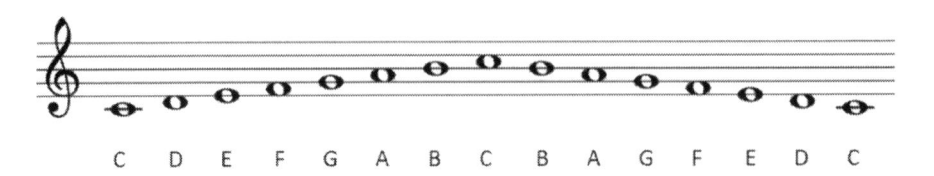

C   D   E   F   G   A   B   C   B   A   G   F   E   D   C

How to play a basic chord on a diatonic harmonica.

When using a ten-hole diatonic harmonica in the key of C major it is evident that exhalation along the instrument results in the playing of notes C, E and G on the diatonic scale. Remember that this combination of these three notes already makes up the root chord of C major. This makes it very easy for us as harmonica players to play the root chord of C on our diatonic harmonica in the key of C major. Inhalation along the instrument results in the playing of notes A, B, D and F which completes the rest of the diatonic scale. Ordering these notes together and playing specific notes simultaneously with the tongue block technique will result in you playing a chord. The way the harmonica holes have been tuned and placed helps the player easily play the chords they desire. If you have a ten-hole diatonic harmonica you can try using the picture below to play holes together and create some chords. Write down these chords if you like the way they sound and practice them often.

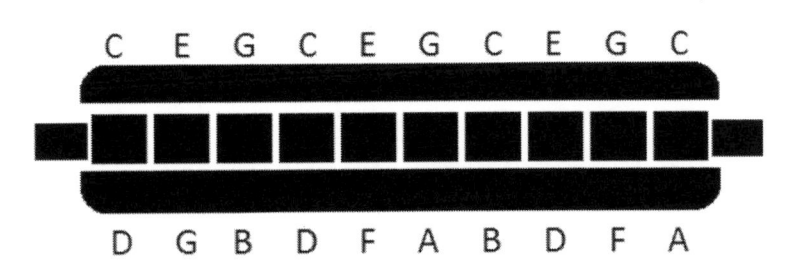

Exhale

```
C  E  G  C  E  G  C  E  G  C
```

```
D  G  B  D  F  A  B  D  F  A
```

Inhale

How to play a chord on a chromatic harmonica.

Chromatic harmonicas follow the chromatic scale which has 12 different pitches.

The chromatic scale still basis its scale off of the diatonic scale but has added notes which sit between notes in the diatonic scale. The chromatic scale ascends and descends with the use of half-steps, known as semi-tone intervals unlike ascending and descending intervals of whole-tones seen in the diatonic scale. These semi-tones or half-steps are identified as sharp (#) or flat (b) variants of notes in the diatonic scale. These semi-tones appear in the middle of two whole notes and can be named after one or the other. The semi-tone is called a sharp if using the note lower in pitch, and a flat if using the note higher in pitch. For example C – D is a whole step with the half note in between either being called C# or Db, resulting in C – C#/Db – D C# and Db are still the same pitched notes and will sound the same.

Having these extra pitches to work with means that there are more scales, resulting in more playable chords.

A chromatic scale in the key of C major would go as follows. Take note of how many notes there are in this scale but remember that the sharps and flats (C#/Db for example) represent one note.

C -- C#/Db -- D -- D#/Eb -- E -- F -- F#/Gb -- G -- G#/Ab - A -- A#/Bb – B.Chromatic harmonicas are able to play a lot more chords than a diatonic harmonica can but the idea and technique behind it are practically the same.

Now that you should have a good idea of what a chord is, let us go back to looking at the technique using the tongue to play chords.

Compacted chord tongue block.

A tongue block - the same technique used for playing single notes – can be used to play a chord by blocking holes that do not sound out the notes a player wishes to include in the chord.

Sometimes playing a chord means using holes that are right next to each other or in other words, a compact chord. This means that the harmonica player can take advantage of this easy positioning of holes and simply block the remaining holes with their tongue.

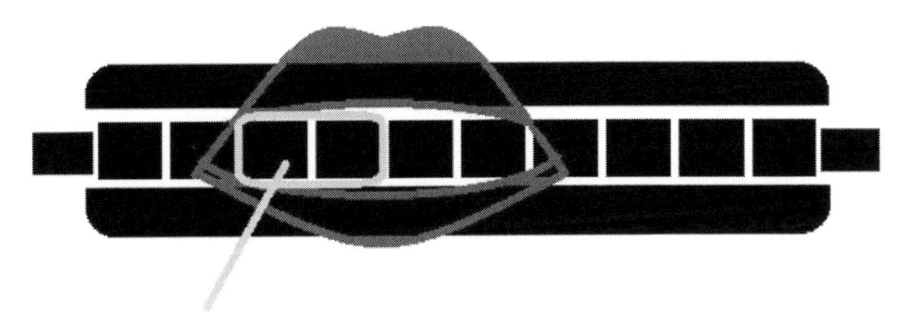

Tongue

This is more often seen with diatonic harmonicas which are in a set scale that allows chord notes to be positioned closely together and played easily. This usually means that most of the holes played will sound good when played together. The chromatic harmonica is slightly more extensive when it comes to playing chords as chords from a variety of keys can be played. Playing a chord with notes sitting next to each other on the harmonica is easily played with the tongue block. The idea behind the tongue block is to simply block all the other holes that are not required to play the chord when the notes for your chord sit next to each other.

Split chord tongue block.

Sometimes it is common to find chords which are made up of notes that are not together on the harmonica – this is called a chord split. This usually means that there are holes that lie in-between holes which should not be played. By placing these unwanted holes in the middle of your mouth you can block them with your tongue and use the side pockets of your mouth to deliver air to the holes that are needing it. Take a look at the illustration below for a better understanding and give it a try yourself.

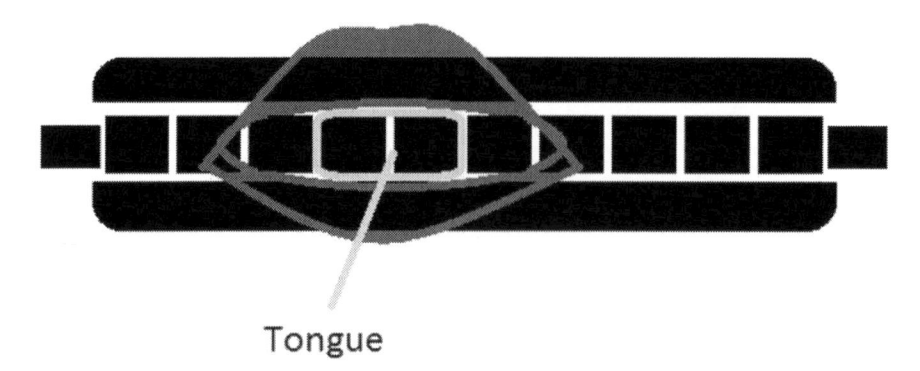

Tongue

Enhancing the Sound with Your Tongue

We have seen from the previous section that the tongue is used for blocking when playing single notes and chords on the harmonica but it also has quite a few other uses. There are many techniques involving the tongue that can be used to enhance the sound of the instrument. Here are a few of the basic ones which you can practice in your own time.

The tongue lift.

The tongue lift is a technique which can beef up the sound of a melody played on the harmonica by adding chords. This technique is a transition technique between a single note and a chord. To use a tongue lift the harmonica player must follow these steps.

- Firstly play a single note on your harmonica using the tongue block method (picture A).

- Now you can simply lift your tongue off of the holes you were blocking to play a chord (picture B). This chord includes your original single note and the holes you were originally blocking.

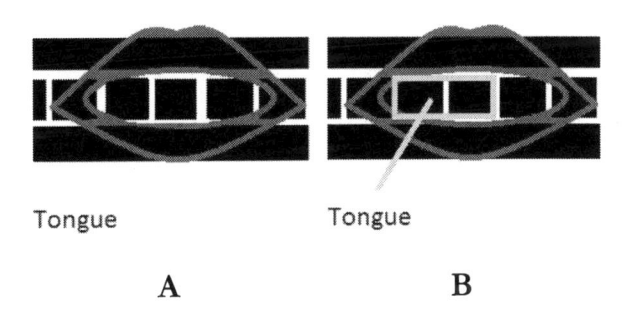

Tongue   Tongue

A   **B**

The tongue slap.

A tongue slap is a technique which helps the player change from a chord to a single note. This technique adds a bit of body to the single note which is played after a fuller sounding chord. To use a tongue slap the harmonica player must follow these steps.

- Firstly play a chord on your harmonica (picture A). Remember that a chord is two or more single notes being played together.

- Now slap your tongue onto the notes/holes in your chord that you wish to block and isolate a single note/hole on your harmonica (picture B).

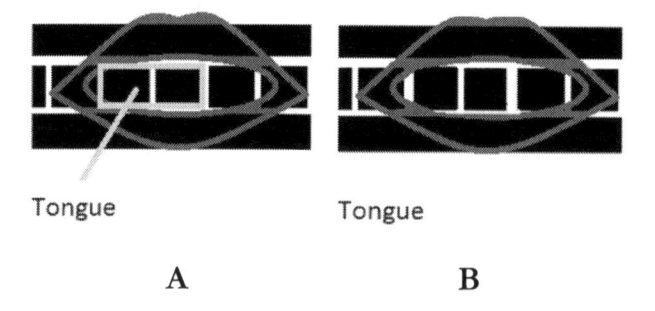

Tongue   Tongue

A   B

This is how you successfully play a tongue slap on the harmonica.

You can practice both the tongue slap and the tongue lift by playing different chords and isolating different notes within those chords.

The tongue rake.

The tongue rake is also called a chord rake because of the use of multiple notes. The idea is to use your tongue to slide up and down the holes, you are focusing on in order to create an ascending and descending effect with those few notes. This technique has a very similar sound to that of strumming a guitar and requires at least three holes to work. In order to play a tongue rake one can follow these steps.

- Begin with your mouth creating space to allow airflow to four holes. Begin by blocking one or two of the closest holes on your left with your tongue while leaving the three or two on your right open (picture A).

- Begin to play and continuously move your tongue along the harmonica from side to side until you hear a clear descent and ascent of notes. Look at the pictures A, B, and C below to understand the placement of the tongue for this technique.

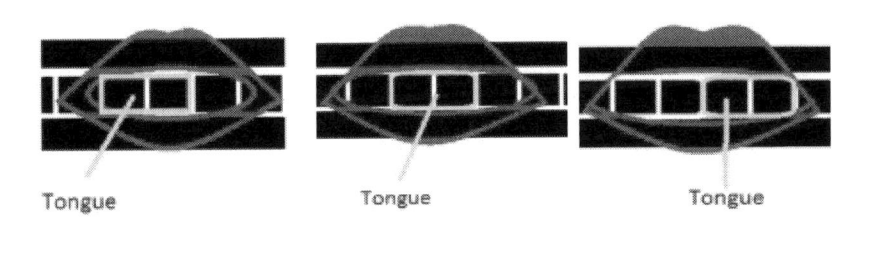

Tongue   Tongue   Tongue

     A   B   C

The pull off.

A pull off is very similar to a tongue lift as it begins with the blocking of holes for a single note and ends with a chord. The difference is that a pull off also involves the blocking of all holes for an instant before playing the chord. This action produces a percussive sound to the change between the single note and chord. To use the pull off a harmonica player must follow these steps

- Firstly play a single note on your harmonica using the tongue block method (picture A).

- Before removing your tongue quickly cover all the holes which are open to airflow with your tongue to block all sound from being produced (picture B).

- Now you can lift your tongue off of the holes you are blocking to play the final chord (picture C)

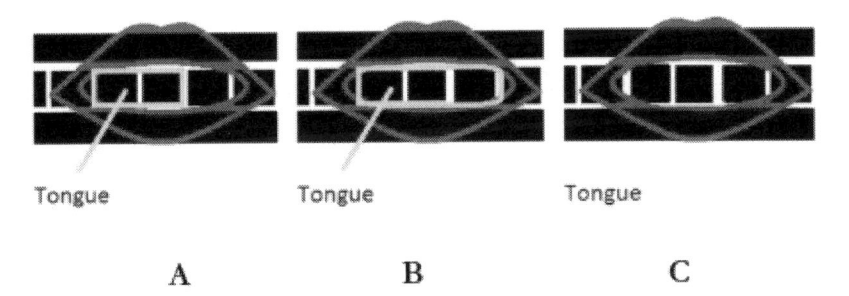

A   B   C

The chord hammer.

The chord hammer is a technique where the harmonica player repeatedly lifts and replaces their tongue on certain holes of the harmonica. The chord hammer gets its name from the nature of its action – the tongue almost acts as a hammer, repeatedly hammering away at the holes focused on. The reason why the word 'chord' is included is because of the chord produced during the hammer. The lifting of the tongue during the hammer creates a chord which compliments the single note or chord it sits on. A harmonica player can follow these steps to play and practice their chord hammer.

- Firstly, try to play a single note using the tongue block technique (picture A).

- Now lift the tongue and quickly produce a chord (picture B). Replace your tongue after a short moment (picture C) and repeat with rhythm to achieve a hammering effect.

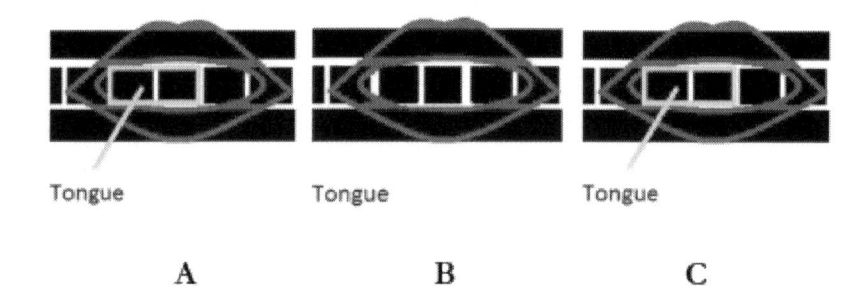

Tongue   Tongue   Tongue

A   **B**   **C**

The shimmer.

The shimmer is probably one of the harder techniques of the tongue. This is because it requires more tongue control which can be difficult at first for some harmonica players. The shimmer begins with a tongue block leaving airflow to one hole at the end of your mouth. The idea is to repeatedly alternate the airflow from the hole on your far left of your mouth to the hole on your far right and vice versa. Only the notes at the end of each side of your mouth should be played repeatedly with rhythm to create a shimmering effect. You can achieve this by pressing the tip of your tongue against the harmonica in the middle of the two notes. Then by leaning your tongue from side to side, opening and closing holes to alternate from note to note repeatedly. You can make this easier by learning the harmonica from side to side with you if you are battling to open and close those two holes on the end.

Look at picture A and then B and C below to fully understand the technique.

These are some of the main techniques that a harmonica player can use to enhance the sound with their tongue. You can use these explanations and illustrations to practice on your own at home. Try mixing a few together in a sequence of a few chords or notes to make it more exciting. Remember to take it at your own pace and work on these techniques to develop muscle memory and your skill.

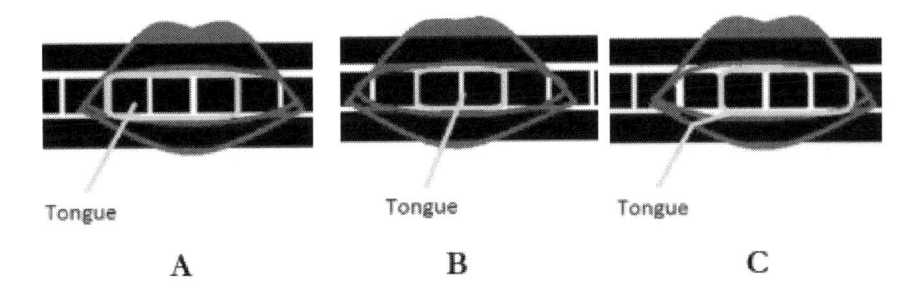

A

B

C

Bending the Notes

What is a bend on the harmonica?

A bend on the harmonica is usually found in the genres of rock, pop, blues, country, and jazz. The technique is widely used as a form of expression on the harmonica and can often produce a sound that conveys a type of emotion. A bend is a smooth transition from the original note into the bendable note and can often sound like wailing. It is an advanced technique that could take some time to learn but the benefits of knowing how to bend are priceless.

How does bending work?

The reeds in a harmonica are all set to play one pitch using their own vibrations from your breath. These reeds can be altered in pitch by making them vibrate faster or slower. This can be done through using certain techniques inside and around the mouth. Some play the harmonica at a slight angle to help with bending their notes but this is not a must. Bending can be done during inhalation and exhalation and it is advisable to practice both to develop the technique properly.

Bending is possible mainly through the correct shaping inside a harmonica players mouth. A beginner should begin practicing bending through one hole, using one note at a time. This means that you can use either the tongue block method or the pucker method to isolate a note, it is up to you. Just remember to choose the one you feel comfortable with but do not close off any

Bending the Notes

options.

Some holes bend well during inhalation and others during exhalation, it is up to you to play around with your harmonica and take this information given to you to figure it out. For the purpose of this section, we will focus on a ten-hole diatonic harmonica in the key of C to understand the idea behind bending a note.

The holes to bend during inhalation on a ten-hole diatonic harmonica in the key of C major are holes one, two, three, four and six. The holes to bend during exhalation on the same harmonica are holes eight, nine and ten. Holes five and seven are not easily bendable and are often ignored. Some holes are able to bend up to one and a half steps/tones depending on the extremity of the shaping of the mouth. Take a look at the picture below to see the extent to which these holes bend.

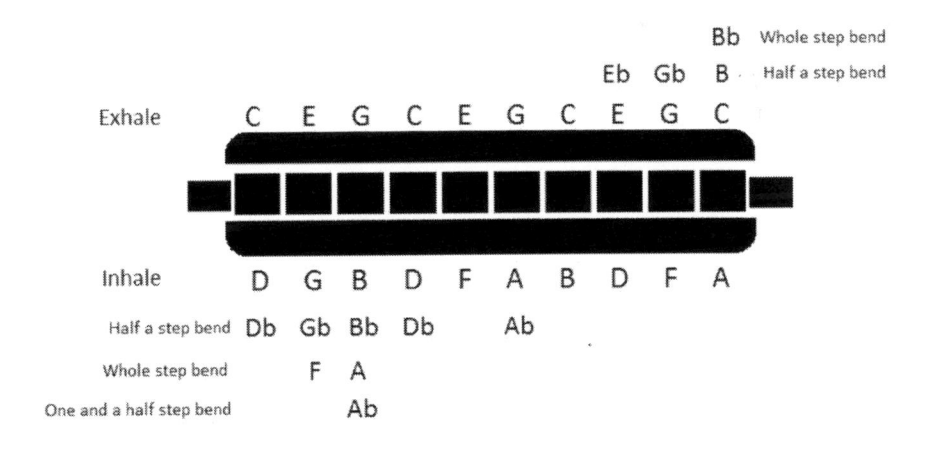

										Bb	Whole step bend
								Eb	Gb	B	Half a step bend
Exhale		C	E	G	C	E	G	C	E	G	C
Inhale		D	G	B	D	F	A	B	D	F	A
Half a step bend	Db	Gb	Bb	Db		Ab					
Whole step bend		F	A								
One and a half step bend			Ab								

Bending during inhalation.

Before grabbing your harmonica and trying to bend it is important to get the shape of your mouth correct first. Bending during inhalation requires the same shape of mouth used when imitating the sound of a donkey. This sound is pronounced EEE – AWE. The EEE sound keeps the jaw quite close together and closes the passage of air traveling out of the mouth. The AWE sound uses a dropped jaw and open mouth to produce a fuller sound with more air traveling out of the mouth.

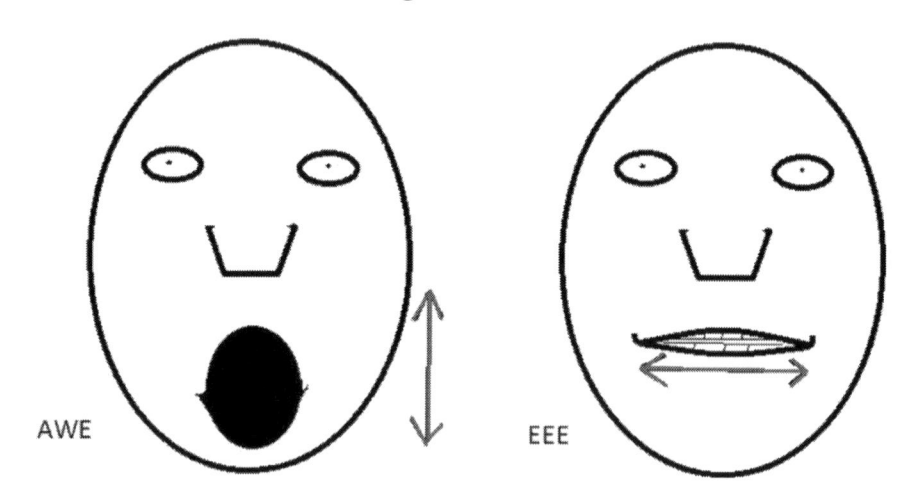

AWE   EEE

Remember that the holes to bend during inhalation on a ten-hole diatonic harmonica in the key of C are holes one, two, three, four and six.

Now you can grab your harmonica. Correctly grip your harmonica and isolate a hole that will bend during inhalation. After you have picked your hole you can inhale until you stabilize the sound of your note. Now try shaping your mouth from a natural EEE to AWE.

You may not get it at first but keep trying as it is a technique that requires more practice time than others.

Focus on the shape of your mouth and visualize a drop in pitch. Visualizing is an important aspect in developing your muscle memory around your mouth as we need to mentally make the connections to these new physical movements until they become natural to us. Move around your harmonica and bend as much as you can while inhaling

Bending during exhalation.

Bending during exhalation is practically the same as bending during inhalation with the only difference being that you reverse the shaping of your mouth. Instead of shaping your mouth from EEE to AWE, you need to shape your mouth from AWE to EEE resulting in AWE – EEE for exhalation.

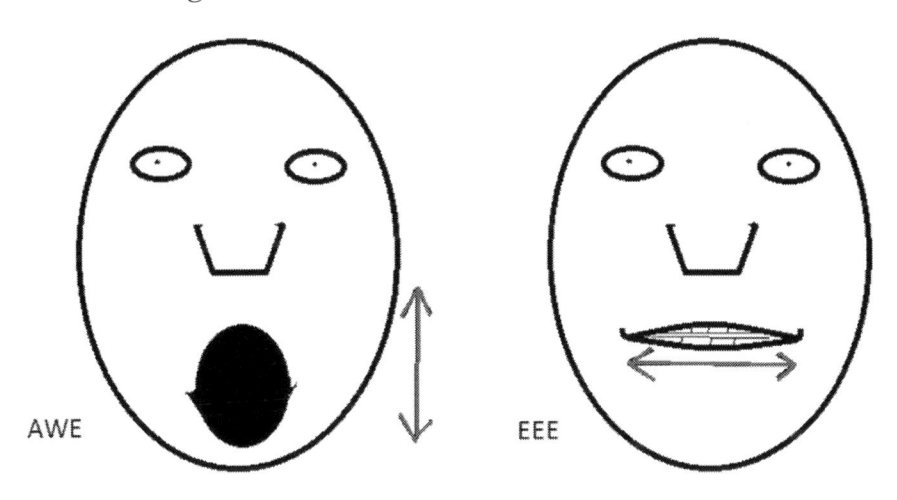

AWE   EEE

Remember that the holes to bend during inhalation on a ten-hole diatonic harmonica, in the key of C, are holes eight, nine and ten.

Once again you can grab your harmonica. Correctly grip your harmonica and isolate a note. After you have picked your hole you can exhale until you stabilize the sound of your note. Now try shaping your mouth with the new AWE to EEE. Focus on the shape of your mouth again and make sure to visualize. Practice by bending all the notes you can on exhale and get familiar with the feel of the action.

Remember that bending is a tough technique to acquire but it will come very naturally once you get the hang of it. Keep working on these bends and get familiar with how your harmonica can bend. This technique is a great one to learn and add to your harmonica playing to give it soul and color.

Playing the Harmonica in Many Keys

By now we should be very familiar with the ten-hole diatonic harmonica in the key of C major. This type of harmonica will be used again as an example to explain how a harmonica can be played in multiple keys. Most harmonicas at least make use of the diatonic scale so the ten-hole diatonic harmonica can be used as a great example. The ten-hole diatonic harmonica in the key of C major has the root note of C and a scale of C – D – E – F – G – A – B. On exhalation the holes one to ten follow the pattern of C – E - G. These three notes make up the root chord of C major which makes it easier for the player to play in the key of C. A harmonica player can play in the key of C by running through their scale on their harmonica, starting at any C found on the harmonica. Note C is found on holes 1, 4, 7 and 10.

You can try playing a scale on your ten-hole diatonic harmonica in the key of C major by using the picture below.

Exhale

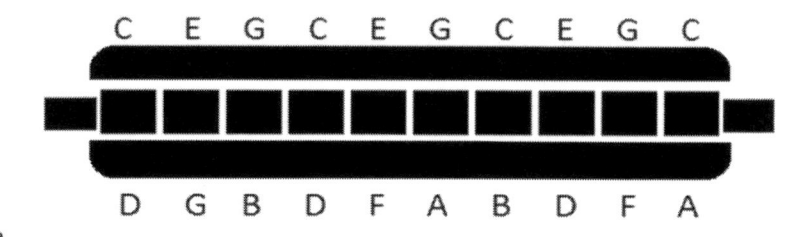

C E G C E G C E G C

D G B D F A B D F A

Inhale

To change the key played on the harmonica a player must simply play from another position on their harmonica and make a new root note for their scale. The harmonica player must play in a different position from that of hole number one and continue the scale in the correct order of pitch. If a musician wanted to play in the key of E major they would make their first/root note E, with the scale being E – F – G –A – B – C - D. Many find it easier to quickly play root chords of the key they have changed too. This is to familiarize themselves with the 1st, 3rd and 5th notes of that new key as these are also notes that are played often to emphasize that new key. Major chords are usually played with three different notes – C major, for example, has a root chord consisting of notes C – E – G as seen as the pattern for exhalation on this harmonica. A root chord for the new key of G would include the notes G – B – D. To figure out the root chord of the scale you include the first, third and fifth note of that scale. The name of the scale defines the root note so you know that C major will always start with a C whereas G major will always begin the scale with a G.

You should first get familiar with where to find all those specific notes on your harmonica before you start experimenting with key change.

Try to use the picture above to map out a few keys such as B major and D major and their root chords to see the patterns of play needed for that key

Here are the seven whole tone keys and their related root chords and scales for you to use. Try practice playing in these different keys and then attempt to play the root chords of these scales. Use the picture on the page before as a reference to see where your notes are on your harmonica. You will find that some chords will be impossible to play so do not worry too much about them.

Scales of keys:

C major = C – D – E – F – G – A – B
D major = D – E – F – G – A – B – C
E major = E – F – G – A – B – C – D
F major = F – G – A – B – C – D – E
G major = G – A – B – C – D – E – F
A major = A – B – C – D – E – F – G
B major = B – C – D – E – F – G – A

Root chord of keys:

C major = C – E – G
D major = D – F – A
E major = E – G – B
F major = F – A – C
G major = G – B – D
A major = A – C – E
B major = B – D – F

These are only keys mainly used in diatonic scales. There are scales which have sharpened or flattened root notes but beginners should stick with these main seven keys and practice their diatonic scale before moving onto the chromatic scale.

Making sure that you change the root note of your scale and abide by the note structure of those scales on your harmonica will help you develop your skill of naturally being able to change key and know where to find those notes. This is a tricky part of harmonica playing as it involves music theory which can be quite daunting to some who have never studied it. It is however straight forward and simple to learn if given the time and effort. Fundamental music theory is learnable through the practice of your instrument and one should not let their lack of knowledge of music theory affect their will to learn.

Bringing It All Together

Now that we have come to the end of the book it should be easy to see how all these topics relate to each other and co-exist or overlap to create the phenomenon that is the sound of the harmonica. These techniques and the information given to you will hopefully guide you into learning the basics of the instrument as well as you can.

This book should have helped you understand the story around the harmonica and how it came about - knowing your instrument is a great way of fueling your inspiration for the music you play on it.

This book has also commented on the different parts that make up a harmonica to help you develop an understanding of how the instrument actually works. Knowing this can also tie in well with your technical work on the harmonica, as you can actually start making the physical connections between yourself and the instrument. After reading this book you should also have a good idea of many different types of harmonicas that can be found as well as knowing how to find and purchase a harmonica that is ideal for you.

This book has also touched on technical aspects such as harmonica grips, playing single notes, playing chords, using tongue techniques, bending notes and playing in different in keys. This book has touched on some music theory related to the harmonica, which is used to help develop practical technique on the instrument.

This summary can help you go back and check what you have learned. All sections in this book dealing with the technicality of the instrument take you through steps that provide a platform for constant practice and exercise. Most explanations are exercises themselves and can be used to practice and develop your technique.

We have now come to the end of the book so here are a few tips you can use to help you develop as a player of the harmonica.

- Make notes of things you are battling with. This way you won't fall behind in skill by forgetting where you were having problems with learning. Knowing your weaknesses are the only way to improve them.

- Listen to music with a harmonica being played in it or listen to harmonica music. Going to watch live artists is a big plus as you can see the skill of playing the harmonica right in front of you. You can also watch videos of live performances by well-known artists.

- Find a good style of harmonica playing you enjoy. Finding a genre can help inspire you to learn as well as give you a taste of what you can do on your instrument. Listening to harmonica music you enjoy will also help you identify techniques used in that genre. Listen to details of the music to help identify the techniques used.

- Find a good harmonica player as a role model. Having a favorite artist or artists (especially a current one) can keep you in the loop with the new trends or fads happening with the instrument. Music is forever evolving and keeping up with the times is a new way to develop your technique.

Printed in Great Britain
by Amazon